NATIONAL GEOGRAPHIC
KiDS

Ick!

DELIGHTFULLY DISGUSTING ANIMAL DINNERS, DWELLINGS, AND DEFENSES

MELISSA STEWART

NATIONAL GEOGRAPHIC
WASHINGTON, D.C.

TABLE OF CONTENTS

INTRODUCTION

DON'T BE TOO QUICK TO SAY "ICK!"

EATING POOP. BUILDING A HOME FROM SPIT. SQUIRTING BLOOD AT ENEMIES. To us, these animal activities seem shocking. After all, people invented toilets and tissues so we could get rid of gross, gooey, stinky stuff ASAP (as soon as possible). That way, we'd hardly have to think about it at all.

But here's a surprise: Some animals do things that we think are yucky. They dine on dung or vomit or fingernail clippings. They live in slimy snot or rotting carcasses. To protect themselves from predators, they fling feces, roll in pee, or blast blood at their enemies. Yep, it's true.

Want to know more? Then you're in for a treat! This book is chock-full of disgusting details, so turn the page and start reading.

IMAGINE...

EATING YOUR MOM'S WARM, STINKY POOP. If you were a baby panda, you'd gobble it up lickety-split.

IMAGINE…

BUILDING A NEST OUT OF STICKY STRANDS OF DRIED SALIVA. If you were a white-nest swiftlet, you'd scout out a spot and start spitting.

IMAGINE…

SQUIRTING BLOOD OUT OF THE CORNERS OF YOUR EYES to scare off a schoolyard bully. If you were a Texas horned lizard, you'd take aim and … *whoosh!*

Introduction **7**

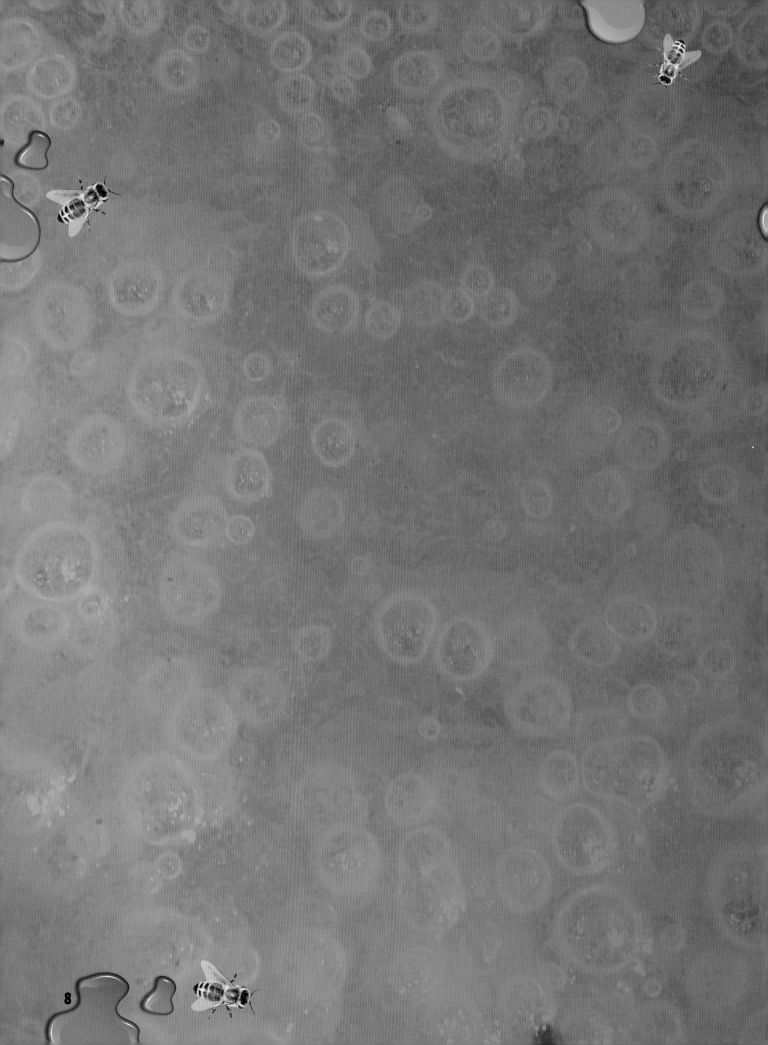

DISGUSTING DINNERS

YOU WON'T BELIEVE WHAT SOME ANIMALS EAT!

a honeybee with a drop of nectar

EASTERN COTTONTAIL RABBIT

THOSE RASCALLY RABBITS

EASTERN COTTONTAIL RABBITS MAY LOOK CUTE and cuddly, but they have a nasty habit: They eat their own droppings.

Most of the time, rabbits eat grass. Lots of it. And grass is hard to digest. So once a day, they produce cecotropes (see-KO-tropz)—soft, shiny pellets full of partially digested food.

A rabbit can't resist these poopy pellets. It scarfs them down while they're still warm. *Eww!*

As cecotropes travel through a rabbit's digestive system, the bacteria in its intestines get another opportunity to break down the grass and absorb important nutrients. Finally, the rabbit produces a set of hard fecal droppings, which it doesn't eat.

STAT STACK

Habitat: Grasslands, open woodlands

Size: 14 to 19 inches (36 to 48 cm) long

Weight: 2 to 4 pounds (0.9 to 1.8 kg)

Predators: Snakes, coyotes, cougars, foxes, weasels, eagles, hawks, owls

Life span: 5 years

What would you do if your front teeth grew nonstop? Rabbits gnaw on bark and twigs to wear down their out-of-control choppers.

🤔 Two Types of Teeth

Snip, snip, clip. A rabbit slices and dices plant parts with its incisors—long front teeth that never stop growing. The cuddly critter also has wide, flat molars. These back teeth crush and grind food before the rabbit gulps it down.

🤢 EXTRA ICK!

Believe it or not, rabbits aren't the only critters that chow down cecotropes. Guinea pigs, hares, and capybaras eat them, too.

capybara

AN EASTERN COTTONTAIL EATS CECOTROPES EVERY DAY. By digesting its food twice, the rabbit gets an extra supply of the vitamins, minerals, proteins, and sugars it needs to live and grow.

GIANT PANDA

ALL IN THE FAMILY

A FEMALE GIANT PANDA gives birth inside a cave or hollow tree. And she stays there with her cub for up to four months. During that time, the little one gets all the energy it needs to grow by drinking milk from its mama's body.

Before the cub can eat solid food, it needs to dine on its mom's dung. Why eat poop? Because it's full of bacteria. The baby panda needs bacteria in its own body to digest bamboo.

Believe it or not, a mother panda eats poop, too. In fact, the little one won't poop or pee unless the mama licks its bottom. By swallowing her baby's smelly waste, the mother keeps her cub safe. After all, if a hungry snow leopard catches the scent of a young panda, it will attack.

STAT STACK

Habitat: Forests with bamboo

Size: 6 feet (1.8 m) long

Weight: 250 pounds (113 kg)

Predators: Jackals, snow leopards, yellow-throated martens

Life span: 20 years

A giant panda cub BEGINS EATING BAMBOO WHEN IT'S ABOUT SIX MONTHS OLD, but it stays with its mom for up to two years.

🤔 What's That Sound?

Giant pandas live in thick forests, so they usually can't see one another. How do they stay in touch? By making all kinds of calls. They bark, moan, huff, honk, growl, and squeal to let other pandas know where they are, what they're doing, and how they feel.

A newborn panda is tiny. Its eyes are shut, and it has no teeth or fur. When a panda cub wants its mama's attention, it whimpers.

😷 EXTRA ICK!

Most mammals produce brown poop—just like you. But a giant panda's scat is green and stringy. Why do the droppings look a lot like bamboo, a panda's favorite food? Because a panda's body has a hard time digesting the tough plants.

RED-SPOTTED PURPLE BUTTERFLY

SLURPING UP SUPPER

MANY BUTTERFLIES EAT JUST ONE THING: flower nectar. They can't get enough of the sweet stuff.

But red-spotted purple butterflies prefer a different kind of meal—and they aren't alone. At least seven kinds of butterflies sip juices from rotting fruit, animal dung, and dead animal bodies. *Blech!*

Why in the world would butterflies choose such curious cuisine? Because the juices are packed with nutrients the butterflies need to stay healthy. In fact, some scientists think the females can't produce eggs until they've sucked up these vile vittles.

STAT STACK

Habitat: Open woods, forest edges

Size: 3 inches (7.6 cm) across

Weight: Less than 1 ounce (less than 30 g)

Predators: Birds, frogs, lizards, spiders

Life span: Less than 1 year

When a red-spotted purple caterpillar is fully grown, it may weigh 1,000 times more than when it hatched.

🤔 Disguised as Dung

A red-spotted purple caterpillar doesn't eat dung, but it sure looks like the stinky stuff. The disgusting disguise helps the little larva stay safe from hungry birds.

As the caterpillar gorges on leaves, its body grows and grows. Eventually, its hard exoskeleton splits open and the larva sheds its skin. What does the caterpillar do next? It eats some more. It keeps on growing and molts four more times before finally becoming a pupa (PEW-pah).

PROBOSCIS

A red-spotted purple butterfly **SIPS JUICES FROM A ROTTING PERSIMMON FRUIT THROUGH ITS PROBOSCIS**—a long, thin tube that works like a drinking straw. When mealtime is over, the butterfly rolls up its mega-mouthparts and flits away.

🤢 EXTRA ICK!

You won't believe the gross grub some butterflies suck and slurp. Their liquid diet can include everything from mud and blood to tears and sweat. A few even sip their own urine. Yuck!

butterfly sucking up mud

TURKEY VULTURE

A HELPFUL HEAD

COULD A TURKEY VULTURE WIN first prize in a beauty contest? Probably not. But its ugly bald head comes in handy at feeding time.

For starters, the super sensors inside the bird's nostrils work with its brain to detect tiny amounts of ethyl mercaptan, a gas that dead animals give off when they start to rot. While flying high above the ground, a turkey vulture has no trouble picking up the scent of the stinky gas coming from its next meal.

As the bird chows down, it may stick its whole head inside the carcass to reach the morsels of meat. The sticky, smelly flesh would cling to feathers, but it slides right off a bald head. That helps the turkey vulture stay clean.

STAT STACK

Habitat: Open woodlands, scrublands, pastures, deserts

Size: 25 to 32 inches (64 to 81 cm) long

Weight: 2 to 5 pounds (1 to 2.3 kg)

Predators: Skunks, owls, raccoons, hawks, bobcats, snakes

Life span: 16 years

The white streak on this turkey vulture's leg is uric acid, a chemical in its waste products.

🤔 Keeping Cool

On hot days, you cool off by sweating. A dog beats the heat by panting. What does a turkey vulture do? It relieves itself—on its legs.

Sounds gross, right? But human sweat, dog drool, and vulture waste have something in common: They all contain water. As the water evaporates, or turns into a gas that rises into the air, our bodies lose some of its heat.

A turkey vulture has a **BETTER SENSE OF SMELL THAN OTHER BIRDS OF PREY.** It often finds a carcass first, and other birds of prey follow it to the feast.

🤢 EXTRA ICK!

If something startles a turkey vulture while it's eating, the bird upchucks its meal—sometimes right into the carcass. Vomiting its vittles decreases the vulture's body weight, so it can take flight quickly.

BLACK-BACKED JACKAL

PUPS THAT LOVE PUKE

ONE THING'S FOR SURE: Black-backed jackals aren't picky eaters. They'll attack anything from rats and snakes to birds and insects. They'll devour fruit, too.

And that's not all. Jackals don't let anything go to waste. They're happy to eat the meat lions, leopards, and other predators leave behind—even if it's swarming with maggots and has been rotting for days.

When a mama jackal is so full she can't eat another bite, she hurries back to her den. As soon as she sees her hungry pups, she regurgitates, or throws up, her last meal as partially digested mush. Then the little ones greedily lap up the putrid puke. *Yum!*

STAT STACK

Habitat: Woodlands, savannas

Size: 15 to 20 inches (38 to 51 cm) at the shoulder

Weight: 15 to 30 pounds (6.8 to 13.6 kg)

Predators: Leopards, hyenas, eagles

Life span: 10 to 12 years

A female black-backed jackal usually gives birth to three or four pups at a time. Luckily, her mate and older pups help feed the little ones.

🤔 Why Regurgitate?

Believe it or not, lots of animals barf for their babies. Why do wolves, foxes, harvest mice, and many kinds of birds go to all that trouble? Regurgitating makes sense when:
1. Prey is too big to carry back to an animal's den or nest.
2. Predators might try to steal prey dangling from a parent's mouth.

🤢 EXTRA ICK!

Ever noticed the red mark near the tip of an adult gull's beak? When chicks peck that spot, a parent opens its mouth and upchucks its last meal.

Black-backed jackal pups **EAT VOMITED VITTLES,** like the mother is throwing up here, **UNTIL THEY'RE ABOUT SIX MONTHS OLD.**

GERENUK

A FLOOD OF CUD

WHEN YOU SWALLOW YOUR FOOD, it's gone for good. But a gerenuk's dinner goes for a wild ride as the animal's body digests it.

Everything a gerenuk eats surges back up its *looooong* throat two, three, maybe even four times. And each time, the animal chews its cud (partially digested food) a little bit more.

With each re-swallowing, bacteria living in the first two chambers of the gerenuk's stomach get another chance to feast on the flood of cud. They help break it down so it can enter the animal's blood. Eventually, the slushy mush moves through the third and fourth stomach chambers and heads to the intestines, where even more nutrients are absorbed. Finally, the lumpy leftovers exit through the gerenuk's anus. That's right— they're poop.

STAT STACK

Habitat: Semidry bushlands

Size: About 5 feet (1.5 m) long

Weight: Up to 115 pounds (52 kg)

Predators: Cheetahs, leopards, lions, hyenas, jackals

Life span: Up to 8 years

🤔 What a Great Trick!

A gerenuk is only about three feet (1 m) tall at the shoulder, but thanks to its long neck and its ability to balance on its back feet, it can reach tasty leaves more than six feet (2 m) off the ground.

Small groups of female gerenuks often live and feed together.

Many of the trees and bushes a gerenuk eats are covered with sharp, spiky thorns. Its **SNOUT AND MOUTH ARE SMALL, NARROW,** and pointed so the African antelope can avoid getting pricked as it plucks tender leaves off plants.

😷 EXTRA ICK!

Think gerenuks are the world's only cud chewers? Think again. Cattle, goats, sheep, and deer are all ruminants. So are buffalo, wildebeests, and giraffes. In fact, more than 150 kinds of plant-eating mammals re-munch their lunch.

blue wildebeest

Disgusting Dinners **21**

HONEYBEE

WHAT'S IN YOUR HONEY?

YOU PROBABLY KNOW THAT HONEYBEES make sweet, sticky honey. But do you know how? Well, you're about to find out, and the process might surprise you.

1. A field bee—a honeybee that leaves the hive to collect nectar—sucks up thin, runny liquid from dozens of flowers. She swallows some of the nectar and stores the rest in her honey sac.

2. Back at the hive, the field bee upchucks the nectar, and a house bee slurps it into her honey sac. Little by little, she regurgitates the sugary stuff. As she rolls it around in her mouth, it mixes with her spit. The nectar warms up and thickens.

3. After the house bee spreads the mixture along honeycomb cells inside the hive, her sisters fan their wings over the cells. Water evaporates, causing the liquid to thicken even more.

4. After about five days, most honey is ready for the bees to eat. It's nutritious and delicious!

STAT STACK

Habitat: Fields, forests, gardens

Size: Worker: 0.5 inch (1.3 cm) long; queen: 0.8 inch (2 cm) long

Weight: 0.3 ounce (8.5 g)

Predators: Birds, bears, opossums, raccoons, honey badgers, skunks

Life span: Worker: about 6 weeks; queen: up to 5 years

A field bee **STORES DROPS OF NECTAR, LIKE THIS ONE, IN ITS HONEY SAC.** The sac can hold nectar from about 100 flowers. A honeybee typically collects about 10 loads of nectar every day.

Some kinds of bees die each autumn. Others hibernate during the coldest part of the year. But honeybees spend winter feasting on honey and shivering to stay warm inside their hive.

It's Spit-tacular!

Bee spit is a key ingredient of honey. It breaks down the sugars in nectar, making honey easier for bees—and us—to digest. It also helps honey stay fresh for a long time. That's important because honeybees can't collect nectar in the winter.

EXTRA ICK!

What does an archerfish have in common with honeybees? Spit is a part of every meal. The hungry hunter spits at insects, knocking them into the water. Then it swims over and ... *CHOMP!*

BEADED LACEWING

TOXIC TOOTS

A YOUNG BEADED LACEWING LARVA MAY BE TINY, but it has a gigantic appetite. And it has a wicked weapon that can take down its favorite prey—termites that are 35 times heavier.

When the little larva feels the need to feed, it points its rear end at the head of a potential victim and lets one rip. That's right—it farts. The toxic toot stuns the termite. And in less than three minutes, it keels over onto its back.

As the termite struggles to get up, the lacewing scuttles over and plunges its mouthparts into the victim. It injects digestive juices into its prey. Then it waits. Once the termite's guts have turned to mush, the larva slurps them up.

STAT STACK

Habitat: Forests, buildings made of wood

Size: 0.3 inch (8 mm)

Weight: Larvae .00002 ounce (0.6 mg)

Predators: Birds, bats, large insects

Life span: About 3 months

A beaded lacewing larva often **ATTACHES GRASS, PEBBLES, OLD PUPA CASES, AND OTHER MATERIALS TO ITS BACK.** They help the insect hide from predators as it hunts western subterranean termites.

Young beaded lacewings may be horrific hunters, but when they grow up, they dine on plant juices with strawlike mouthparts.

🤔 A Fatal Fart

Female beaded lacewings lay their eggs on wood that's infested with termites. When the larvae hatch, they crawl through cracks and crevices until they find the termites. Then they start to hunt.

A blast of larval gas is powerful enough to paralyze six termites. If the hungry hunter leaves some termites uneaten, the paralyzed victims die about three hours later. Now that's a fatal fart!

🤢 EXTRA ICK!

Beaded lacewing larvae may be famous for their toxic toots, but termites have them beat. Believe it or not, all the termites on Earth pass more than 22 million tons (20 million t) of gas each year! Eating wood makes them tiny fart factories.

VAMPIRE BAT

OUT FOR BLOOD

IT'S HARD TO IMAGINE DINING on nothing but blood, but a vampire bat doesn't mind it a bit. As far as the furry flier is concerned, blood really hits the spot.

The bat uses its razor-sharp teeth to slice open its prey. Then it laps up the bounty of blood. During a 20-minute feeding session, the little bloodsucker drinks about six teaspoons (29 ml) of blood. That may not seem like much, but it's half the bat's body weight!

All that extra body weight would make it hard to fly, but the bat has a trick for lightening its load. It starts to urinate before it even finishes its meal.

STAT STACK

Habitat: Caves in rainforests and deserts

Size: 3.5 inches (9 cm) long

Weight: 2 ounces (57 g)

Predators: Eagles, hawks

Life span: 12 years

🤔 Bats Need Buddies

Vampire bats can't go more than a day or two without food. What happens when an unlucky hunter misses a meal? It licks the lips and fur of a well-fed friend. And its buddy responds by regurgitating part of its last blood meal into the starving bat's mouth. It knows its pal will return the favor another night.

Vampire bats usually roost, or rest, in hollow trees or caves. The more often two bats roost together, the more likely they are to share food.

🤢 EXTRA ICK!

Earth is home to lots of itty-bitty bloodsuckers: Mosquitoes. Bedbugs. Lice and leeches. Most ticks dine on blood, too. One kind of tick lives in caves in Puerto Rico and Cuba. The youngsters greedily gulp the blood of ... bats! The adults gorge on guano (bat poop).

Three kinds of vampire bats feed on blood. The common vampire bat, shown here, usually **ATTACKS COWS, HORSES, AND PIGS.** Hairy-legged vampires and white-winged vampires prefer bird blood.

RED-BILLED OXPECKER

FRIEND OR FOE?

FOR YEARS, PEOPLE THOUGHT RED-BILLED OXPECKERS were doing wildebeests, rhinoceroses, and other large African mammals a big favor by plucking troublesome ticks out of their skin. But now we know better.

It turns out that an oxpecker targets ticks *after* the pests have attacked a mammal and are bursting with blood. That's no help to the mammal!

Why don't oxpeckers eat the ticks sooner? Because they have an appetite for blood—not ticks. And they'll get their favorite food any way they can. That includes picking at a mammal's wounds and sores to keep them bleeding. Gross!

STAT STACK

Habitat: Savannas

Size: 8 inches (20 cm) long

Weight: 2 ounces (57 g)

Predators: None

Life span: 15 years

A red-billed oxpecker **SNACKS ON A TICK FILLED WITH BLOOD** in Kruger National Park in South Africa.

🤔 A Tree-Hole Home

Red-billed oxpeckers may spend most of their time riding atop large mammals, but they build their nests in a pretty typical spot—inside a tree hole. To make it cuddly-cozy, the birds line it with hair they've plucked from their mammal hosts.

After the female oxpecker lays her eggs, the proud parents work together to care for their clutch. And when the chicks hatch, they take turns feeding and protecting the little ones.

🤢 EXTRA ICK!

What do red-billed oxpeckers eat when blood is in short supply? They climb into a mammal's ear and nibble its earwax. They also dine on spit, snot, and dandruff.

SCUTTLE FLY

YUM! ANT BRAINS

A SCUTTLE FLY MIGHT LOOK HARMLESS, but it's a fire ant's worst nightmare.

As a fire ant goes about its business, a female fly lands on its back and injects a single egg into its body. The unsuspecting ant doesn't feel a thing.

A tiny maggot hatches the next day. It crawls to the ant's head and starts eating. First it slurps up fluids. Then it wolfs down muscle and nerve tissue. Finally, it devours the ant's brain.

The brainless ant wanders aimlessly—like a zombie—for up to two weeks. Then its head pops off, and the maggot settles into its ant-head home. The larva sheds its exoskeleton and becomes a pupa. About two weeks later, an adult fly emerges and starts looking for a mate.

STAT STACK

Habitat: Various

Size: About 0.1 inch (2.5 mm) long

Weight: About .0008 ounce (23 mg)

Predators: Unknown

Life span: About 7 weeks

This female scuttle fly is **LOOKING FOR THE PERFECT PLACE TO LAY AN EGG.** Which ant will she choose?

🤔 The Name Game

Like other flies, the scuttle fly is an aeronautical acrobat. It can dart up, down, and even backward. But when danger threatens, it does something surprising. Instead of escaping into the air, it scuttles, or runs away with herky-jerky motions. That's how the little fly got its name.

Some people prefer to call a scuttle fly a "humpback fly" because its thorax seems to sit on top of its abdomen.

🤢 EXTRA ICK!

The scuttle flies that attack fire ants are part of a large family called Phorid flies. Other kinds of Phorid flies target wasps, bees, earthworms, snails, spiders, centipedes, and millipedes. That's a whole lot of real-life zombies!

GERMAN COCKROACH

NIBBLING ON NAILS

A GERMAN COCKROACH ISN'T A PICKY EATER. It'll greedily gobble all kinds of grub. Cookie crumbs stuck under a couch cushion? Check. Vegetable peelings in the kitchen garbage can? Check. Dry dog food spilled in a cabinet? Check. A moldy french fry underneath the oven? Check.

But cockroach cuisine doesn't stop there. If food scraps are hard to find, the pesky pests get creative. They'll dine on paper, wood, leather, and wallpaper glue. They'll snack on soap, makeup, and used tissues. And, yes, it's true, they'll even nibble on fingernail clippings on the bathroom floor. Now that's disgusting!

 **STAT STACK**

Habitat: Dark corners and crevices of buildings

Size: 0.5 inch (1 to 1.5 cm) long

Weight: Unknown

Predators: Frogs, lizards

Life span: Less than 1 year

🤔 Off With Its Head!

What happens to a cockroach if it loses its head? Not much.

A cockroach controls many body functions, including running, with nerves in its thorax, not its brain. It takes in oxygen through tiny holes on the sides of its body.

No food, no problem—at least for a while.

So what finally does in the beheaded bug? After about a week, it dies of dehydration. Without a mouth, it can't drink.

SPIRACLE

A cockroach has 10 spiracles—holes that take in oxygen—on each side of its body. Five spiracles are visible in this photo.

Cockroaches have lived on Earth for at least 140 million years. What's the secret to their success? Not only will **THEY EAT ALMOST ANYTHING,** but they can survive for weeks with no food at all.

😖 EXTRA ICK!

Would cockroaches ever munch on fingernails that are still attached to a person? Yes—if there's a huge number of roaches and very little food.

In the past, sailors on long voyages sometimes wore gloves to bed so hungry cockroaches wouldn't gnaw on their nails while they were sleeping. Better safe than sorry.

CAECILIAN

MUNCHING ON MOM

EVER PEEL SKIN OFF a roasted chicken and pop it into your mouth? It's pretty tasty, right? But just imagine what it'd be like to rip skin off your mom's belly and gobble it down. That's what little skin-eating caecilians (seh-SILL-yens) do.

A female skin-eating caecilian lays eggs in an underground nest and wraps her body around them. When the little ones hatch, they take turns drinking the clear fluid oozing out of her butt.

Every few days, the youngsters swarm over their mom's body. They scrape her skin with their tiny teeth and gulp it down. Then she grows a new layer of fatty, nutritious skin, and they repeat the rampage.

STAT STACK

Habitat: Tropical rainforests

Size: 6 to 7 inches (15 to 18 cm) long

Weight: 0.1 ounce (2.8 g)

Predators: Unknown

Life span: 13 years

About 200 species of caecilians live on Earth. Most of them look like the ones shown here. Every few days, **YOUNG SKIN-EATING CAECILIANS USE THEIR 44 TINY TEETH TO SHRED THEIR MOTHER'S SKIN.**

CAECILIAN

EARTHWORM

Earthworms are a caecilian's favorite food. The oddball amphibians also eat termites, crickets, and ants.

🤔 On the Hunt

After feeding on its mom for about a month, a young caecilian starts to catch its own food. When an earthworm pokes its body into a caecilian's burrow, the hungry hunter grabs the prey with its teeth. Then it spins in circles to pull the worm's entire body into the tunnel before the prey can escape. What a great trick!

🤢 EXTRA ICK!

A caecilian's closest relatives are frogs and salamanders. When a frog sheds its skin, it pulls the thin covering over its head like it's taking off a sweater. Then the frog shoves the old skin into its mouth and swallows it down.

BLACK LACE-WEAVER SPIDER

GOOD TO THE LAST DROP

MOST FEMALE SPIDERS lay their eggs and then walk away. But a female black lace-weaver spider does everything she can to help her youngsters survive.

When the itty-bitty spiderlings burst into the world, she lays dozens of special eggs to feed them. After about a week, the eggs run out. That's when the mother spider makes the ultimate sacrifice.

She taps on her web to get her youngsters' attention. As they scurry toward her, she presses her body into the crowd, and the spiderlings' hunting instincts kick in. They attack their mom and eat her alive, draining every last drop of fluid from her body.

STAT STACK

Habitat: Fields, forests, basements

Size: 0.6 inch (1.5 cm) long

Weight: Unknown

Predators: Birds, large insects

Life span: Unknown

A female black lace-weaver spider builds webs, like the one shown here. After she dies, her spiderlings live together on the web for about a month. By then, they're big enough to survive on their own.

This female black lace-weaver spider is **GUARDING HER TWO-WEEK-OLD SPIDERLINGS.** Soon they will devour her.

🤔 It Takes a Team

What do black lace-weaver spiderlings do after devouring their mom? They stick together. They hunt as a team so they can attack large insects. When they sense danger, the spiderlings join forces to shake their web. The motion scares away predators who might like a spiderling snack.

🤢 EXTRA ICK!

When desert velvet spiderlings hatch, the start feeding on their mom right away. First, they slurp up the partially digested food inside her stomach. Then they devour her stomach, too. But the family feeding frenzy doesn't stop there. The spiderlings move to the back of their mom's body, pierce her abdomen, and suck the rest of her body dry. Tasty!

SAND TIGER SHARK

SNACKING ON SIBLINGS

YEP, IT'S TRUE. Sand tiger shark brothers and sisters fight to the death. And the winners eat the losers for lunch.

Why doesn't the mama shark stop the bloodbath? Because the battle rages *inside* her body—before the pups are even born.

A female shark produces about 100 eggs and stores them in two compartments in her body. After about five months, the youngsters start hatching. And they're hungry. Very hungry.

What do they eat? Each other. The bigger pups attack their smaller siblings until there are just two sharks left—one in each compartment. Then the victors devour the eggs that haven't hatched.

When the two pups are born, they swim off in opposite directions and begin life on their own.

STAT STACK

Habitat: Coastal waters

Size: Up to 10.5 feet (3.2 m) long

Weight: Up to 350 pounds (159 kg)

Predators: None

Life span: 15 years

🤔 Blasts of Gas!

Most sharks start to sink if they stop swimming, but not a sand tiger shark. When the shark swims near the water's surface, it gulps air. Its stomach blows up like a balloon, helping the fish float.

What happens when the shark wants to dive down? No problem. It burps to get rid of the gas that kept it floating.

A female sand tiger shark produces **A NEW BATCH OF EGGS EVERY TWO TO THREE YEARS.** She may give birth to four or six pups in her lifetime.

A sand tiger shark can dive to a depth of about 600 feet (183 m).

🤢 EXTRA ICK!

When a tiger salamander hatches, it cruises through the water in search of food. If the pond is overcrowded ... *Crash! Bam! Boom!* It keeps accidentally colliding with its siblings. All that body-bumping triggers a surprising change: The tadpole develops a huge head and a wide mouth with long teeth. Then it scarfs down its helpless older siblings until the pond is no longer jam-packed with competitors.

DISGUSTING DWELLINGS

YOU WON'T BELIEVE WHERE SOME ANIMALS LIVE!

This tongue-eating louse lives inside a Clark's anemonefish's mouth.

BURROWING OWL

AN ODOROUS ABODE

SOME BIRDS LINE THEIR NESTS WITH GRASS OR LEAVES. Others use feathers they've plucked out of their bodies. But burrowing owls aren't like other birds. They live in an underground den and line their nest and the areas surrounding it with something surprising—poop.

The owls aren't picky about the source. They'll use any kind of poop they can find.

The stinky scat attracts insects in search of a fecal feast, which means the owls can have a feast of their own—without leaving home. The insects are vital vittles for tiny owlets, but adult owls also eat any small critter they can catch, from spiders and scorpions to mice and lizards.

STAT STACK

Habitat: Grasslands, deserts

Size: 8 to 10 inches (20 to 25 cm) tall

Weight: 5 to 6 ounces (142 to 170 g)

Predators: Hawks, badgers, foxes, bobcats, coyotes

Life span: 8 years

Burrowing owlets stay in their underground nest for about one month. Even after the youngsters are old enough to fly and hunt, their parents help to feed them for another three months.

🤔 What's That Sound?

Burrowing owls raise their young in a den that's been abandoned by ground squirrels. So do rattlesnakes, and the brainy birds use that to their advantage.

If an enemy gets too close, burrowing owls hide in their home. They hiss and make a rattling noise. Those scary snakelike sounds convince most predators to skedaddle.

Most owls are nocturnal, or active at night, but **BURROWING OWLS COME OUT DURING THE DAY.**

🤢 EXTRA ICK!

Splat! What's that gooey white gunk plastered on your car? It's a mixture of pee and poop. But if you compared an owl's pasty waste to another bird's droppings, you'd notice something strange: The owl's has fewer dark chunks of dung. That's because owls, unlike other birds, regurgitate most of the materials their bodies can't digest. An adult burrowing owl upchucks two thumb-size pellets every single day.

burrowing owl pellet

DUNG BEETLE

A FONDNESS FOR FECES

MEET THE DUNG BEETLES—little black insects with a true fondness for feces. They spend most of their time in, on, or under piles of poop.

Some live on top of manure piles. The adults explore the fresh, moist droppings, while the grubs grow in older dung that's drying out.

Others tunnel through dung and build burrows below it. Their cool underground nests keep the poop moist and protect grubs from predators.

The most interesting dung beetles of all sculpt scat into balls and roll their prizes away. When they find a spot with soft soil, they bury the ball. Then females lay eggs in the dung. When the grubs hatch, they're safe and snug ... and surrounded by food!

STAT STACK

Habitat: Deserts, grasslands, forests

Size: 1 inch (2.5 cm) long

Weight: 2 to 5 ounces (57 to 142 g)

Predators: Bats, birds, lizards, foxes

Life span: 3 to 5 years

🤔 What's for Dinner?

When a dung beetle's antennae catch the scent of scat, the insect races toward the source of the stench. The lucky first responders often arrive just 15 seconds after fresh, warm droppings plop on the ground.

Adult dung beetles use their mouthparts to suck or squeeze juices out of the poop. The liquid is full of nutritious bacteria.

A dung beetle is no stranger to hard work. In just one night, it can cart off and bury a supply of poop that weighs 250 times more than its body.

🤢 EXTRA ICK!

Think dung beetles only live far away from humans? Think again. They feed on cow patties on farms and deer droppings in fields or wooded areas.

More than 6,000 species of dung beetles live on Earth. Some can **ROLL BALLS OF POOP** that weigh 50 times more than they do.

AFRICAN MOUND-BUILDING TERMITE

MEGA-MOUNDS

SEE THIS STUNNING STRUCTURE? It was built by a million or more termites smaller than the fingernail on your pinkie. Together, the insects weigh about 33 pounds (15 kg). As they build their home, they may move more than 550 pounds (249 kg) of soil in a year.

How do African mound-building termites hold their home together? With sticky spit *and* poop. It's the perfect self-made glue.

Each termite mega-mound has a network of tunnels that acts like an air-conditioning system. As air moves through the tunnels, it cools the nest below. Dozens of underground rooms are used to store food, hold eggs, and raise young. One special chamber houses the termite queen. She lays hundreds of millions of eggs during her 15-year life.

STAT STACK

Habitat: Savannas

Size: Worker: .14 inch (.36 cm) long; queen: 4 inches (10 cm) long

Weight: Unknown

Predators: Birds, bats, aardvarks, anteaters, pangolins

Life span: Worker: 1 to 2 years; queen: up to 15 years

WORKER

SOLDIER

QUEEN

KING

🤔 A Termite for Every Task

Like bees and ants, termites live in large groups called colonies. Each insect has a job to do.

- **Large workers:** Gather food, repair the outside of the mound
- **Small workers:** Repair the inside of the mound, take care of eggs and nymphs
- **Major soldiers:** Guard the mound's entrance
- **Minor soldiers:** Guard and defend workers
- **Queen:** Lays eggs
- **King:** Leaves the nest to find a mate

Some African mound-building termites construct huge homes, like this one in Ethiopia. **THEY CAN BE 30 FEET (9 M) TALL** and more than 16 feet (5 m) wide.

😫 EXTRA ICK!

Just like African mound-building termites, a little bird called the rufous hornero knows that dirt and dung make great building materials. At nesting time, it piles mud and manure on top of a tree branch. Then it carves out a hole. Over time, the nest dries and hardens in the hot sun.

WHITE-NEST SWIFTLET

BUILT WITH SPIT

YOU'LL NEVER GUESS WHAT WHITE-NEST SWIFTLETS USE TO BUILD THEIR NEST. Dribbles of drool! Really, it's true.

These birds spend hours plastering a cave wall with threads of sticky saliva. As the gummy goo dries, it forms a snug pocket. It's the perfect spot for the female to lay her two white eggs.

After the chicks hatch, their parents work together to care for the little ones. While one guards the nest, the other flies off in search of tasty insects for the whole family. Believe it or not, the strands of spit are more than strong enough to hold the rambunctious youngsters until they're old enough to survive on their own.

STAT STACK

Habitat:	Caves
Size:	4 inches (10 cm) long
Weight:	0.5 ounce (14 g)
Predators:	Owls, snakes, lizards
Life span:	Unknown

Swiftlets aren't the only animals that use echolocation to sense their surroundings. Bats, dolphins, shrews, and oilbirds do, too.

A white-nest swiftlet sits on its **NEST MADE OF SALIVA STRANDS** on the North Andaman Islands in India.

🤔 "Seeing" With Their Ears

As swiftlets chase flying insects, they depend on their eyes to keep track of their prey. But inside dark caves, the birds can barely see a thing. How do they solve this problem? By using echolocation. The swiftlets make clicking sounds, and then they listen. The echoes of their calls tell the birds the size, shape, and location of nearby objects.

🤢 EXTRA ICK!

Would you like to eat swiftlet spit? It's a delicacy in Southeast Asia, where workers climb up cave walls and collect the nests of white-nest swiftlets. They sell the dried drool to chefs who use it to make bird's nest soup. Why slurp strands of swiftlet saliva? Some people believe it helps them stay healthy and live a longer life.

bird's nest soup

TONGUE-EATING LOUSE

A MOUTH AS A HOUSE?

IF THERE WERE A PRIZE FOR THE WORLD'S WORST NAME, the tongue-eating louse just might win. For starters, it isn't a louse. It's an isopod—a hard-shelled critter that has more in common with lobsters than lice. And as for eating tongues ... well, that's an exaggeration.

Here's the truth: The young isopods live inside a fish's gills. When they grow up, they're all males. One lucky male turns into a female and crawls into the fish's mouth. She attaches to its tongue and slurps blood until the tongue withers and falls off. Gross!

What does the pesky parasite do once the tongue is gone? She grabs hold of the stub and becomes the fish's new tongue!

STAT STACK

Habitat: Ocean

Size: 0.5 to 1 inch (1.3 to 2.5 cm) long

Weight: Unknown

Predators: Sharks and other large fish that eat the isopod's host

Life span: Up to 3 years

These annoying isopods attack many kinds of fish, including salmon and snapper. Imagine finding one inside the fish you were planning to eat for dinner. *Yuck!*

🤔 Lots of Legs

Lobsters and crabs have 10 legs. But their relatives, the isopods, have 14. The tongue-eating louse uses tiny claws on its back legs to cling to a fish's tongue.

🤢 EXTRA ICK!

Believe it or not, the tongue-eating louse isn't the only mini monster that attacks fish. It belongs to a family of isopods with nearly 400 species, and they all set their sights on fish. They attach to their host's skin, fins, and gills. Some even bore into a fish's muscles.

Say "aaaah." A fish doesn't have hands, so it can't pull a tongue-eating louse out of its mouth. It may have to **PUT UP WITH THE TINY TRESPASSER** for years.

PUSTULATED CARRION BEETLE

EMPTY EGGSHELLS

MOST BURYING BEETLE MAMAS LAY THEIR EGGS NEAR A DEAD ANIMAL. When the youngsters hatch, they feast on the rotting meat.

But that's not how a pustulated carrion beetle feeds her family. She spends her days searching for a snake nest that's full of eggs. Then she lays her own eggs inside the nest.

When the beetle larvae hatch, they tunnel into the snake eggs and devour the tiny snakelets inside. The developing snakes make a great meal.

What do the beetles do next? They settle into their cozy new homes. The empty eggshells are the perfect place to grow up.

STAT STACK

Habitat: Forests

Size: 1 inch (2.5 cm) long

Weight: Unknown

Predators: Unknown

Life span: 1 year

When a pustulated carrion beetle is fully grown, it emerges from its snake-egg home and flies off in search of a mate.

Most burying beetles use their supersensitive antennae to SNIFF A WHIFF OF DECAYING CARCASSES, but scientists aren't sure how pustulated carrion beetles locate snake eggs, like the one shown here.

🤔 How Many Homes?

A pustulated carrion beetle's favorite target is a black rat snake nest. Each snake lays about a dozen eggs, but the females often nest in groups. That means a single rat snake nest may contain more than 100 eggs.

🤢 EXTRA ICK!

What happens if a snake's nest doesn't have enough eggs to feed and house a female beetle's brood? She kills some of her own offspring. Sounds terrible, right? But it's her way of making sure that at least some of the larvae survive.

BONE-EATING SNOT FLOWER WORM

FLOWERLIKE PLUME

MAIN BODY TUBE

ROOTLIKE STRUCTURE

ONE WEIRD WORM

WOULD YOU WANT TO LIVE INSIDE A ROTTING WHALE CARCASS AT THE BOTTOM OF THE SEA? You would if you were a bone-eating snot flower worm. Yep, that's really its name.

The females spend most of their lives attached to a whalebone. Frilly, flowerlike plumes rise above a snotty mucus ball that covers the worm's main body tube. As the plumes wave through the water, they take in oxygen.

The worm's "roots," which are embedded in the whalebone, ooze acids that break down the bone. Then bacteria living inside the worm's main body tube go to work. They absorb fats, oils, and other tasty treats from the decaying bone, so they—and the worm— get all the nutrients they need to survive.

STAT STACK

Habitat: Ocean

Size: Females: 0.5 inch (1.3 cm); males: microscopic

Weight: Unknown

Predators: Unknown

Life span: Unknown

Scientists from the Monterey Bay Aquarium Research Institute in California, U.S.A., used a deep-diving underwater robot to photograph these bone-eating worms blanketing a whale bone in the Pacific Ocean.

Here's a close-up sneak peek of a **FEMALE BONE-EATING SNOT FLOWER WORM.** The image doesn't show the gooey mass of mucus that surrounds and protects the worm's body.

🤔 At the Whalebone Buffet

Female bone-eating worms blast thousands of eggs into the water. As the larvae float on ocean currents, most become fish food. But a few get lucky and land on a decaying corpse. It's not uncommon for a dead whale to host so many worms that it looks like a shaggy pink carpet.

🤢 EXTRA ICK!

Male bone-eating snot flower worms look nothing like the females. And you won't believe where they live! The itty-bitty boys line the slimy walls of a female's main body tube. She may house dozens of swarming males.

This image of a tiny male bone-eating snot flower worm was taken through a high-powered microscope.

BUSHY-TAILED WOOD RAT

PACKED WITH PEE

SOME PEOPLE COLLECT BASEBALL CARDS.
Others amass stamps or key chains or magnets. But
a bushy-tailed wood rat puts them all to shame.
It stockpiles just about anything you
can think of—from pine cones and
feathers to lost earrings and bottle
caps. The shinier, the better.

What does the little hoarder do with
its trove of treasures? It adds them to
its midden—a giant den made of
sticks, bark, rocks, bones, leaves, and
dung. And what holds the hefty heap
together? Wood rat urine. That's right:
pee. The sticky, stinky stuff cements
the colossal pile of prizes into a single
solid mass.

STAT STACK

Habitat: Forests, grasslands,
scrublands

Size: 11 to 18 inches
(28 to 46 cm) long

Weight: Up to 1.3 pounds
(0.6 kg)

Predators: Black bears,
bobcats, coyotes, hawks,
martens, spotted owls,
weasels

Life span: 2 years

This scientist is studying a 5,900-year-old bushy-tailed wood rat midden at the City of Rocks National Reserve in Idaho, U.S.A.

🤔 In the Midst of a Midden

Inside a midden, crisscrossing tunnels connect a series of rooms. Some rooms are for sleeping and raising young. They contain cup-shaped nests lined with grass. Other rooms are for feeding or storing food.

Some middens are thousands of years old! They've been used by generation after generation of wood rats. By studying the materials in these middens, scientists can discover what plants and animals lived in the area long ago.

🤢 EXTRA ICK!

A wood rat can't see very well, so it leaves a trail of urine droplets everywhere it goes. After a day of feeding on twigs, seeds, and fruit, the little critter sniffs its way home.

A wood rat is a small animal, but **ITS MIDDEN MAY BE UP TO 10 FEET** (3 m) tall.

EYELASH MITE

AT HOME ON HUMANS

LOOK AT THESE ITTY-BITTY BEASTS!
They're long and thin like worms but have eight legs like a spider. What are they? Eyelash mites. They live on and in people's skin—maybe even yours! The truth is, most people have them.

The tiny creepy-crawlies spend a lot of time exploring hair follicles—small sacs that eyelashes, eyebrows, and other facial hairs grow out of. They're also fond of pores—small openings on the surface of your skin. Where else do these mini mites like to hang out? On eyelids, noses, and foreheads. They can be found on cheeks and chins, too.

STAT STACK

Habitat:	Human faces
Size:	Microscopic
Predators:	None
Life span:	A few weeks

🤔 Insect Versus Mite

An insect has three main body parts—a head, a thorax, and an abdomen. It has six legs. A mite is more closely related to spiders, scorpions, and ticks. It has two main body parts—a cephalothorax and an abdomen—and eight legs.

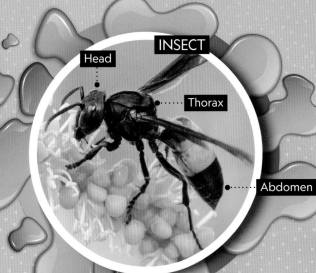

INSECT

Head
Thorax
Abdomen

MITE

Abdomen
Cephalothorax

When hunger hits, eyelash mites, shown here at 1,475 times their actual size, **SLURP UP OILS THAT OOZE OUT OF YOUR SKIN.** They also enjoy chowing down on dead, flaking skin. Ah, what a life!

🤢 EXTRA ICK!

Eyelash mites usually rest during the day. At night, they creep across your face at a super-slow pace, moving just a half inch an hour (1.3 cm/h). Maybe that's one reason you never feel a thing.

ITCH MITE

DIG IN!

GET READY! YOU'RE ABOUT TO MEET SOME CREEPY CRITTERS that will really make your skin crawl. They're itch mites, and they live on—and in—people all over the world.

Male itch mites spend most of their time skittering across the skin's surface, but the females dig down. As they burrow through skin, they suck on body fluids and lay dozens of tiny oval eggs. Their tunnels can be more than an inch (2.5 cm) long.

After the youngsters hatch, they build their own burrows. When they're fully grown, they find mates. Then the females dig down and lay even more eggs.

STAT STACK

Habitat: Humans

Size: Microscopic

Predators: None

Life span: 6 to 9 weeks

Itch mites are so small that you **NEED A MICROSCOPE TO SEE THEM.** The mite in this photo is shown at about 630 times its actual size.

This lumpy, reddish rash is a telltale sign of a scabies infection.

🤔 What's That Rash?

Itch mites can easily spread from person to person. All it takes is a quick handshake.

Unfortunately, itch mites aren't as harmless as eyelash mites. Just 10 or 15 of the tiny troublemakers can cause a red, itchy rash called scabies. Scabies is most common in people's armpits, on their wrists and legs, and between their fingers.

🤢 EXTRA ICK!

As an itch mite sips body fluids and gorges on dead skin, the tasty tidbits travel through its digestive system. What happens to its waste? It shoots out the mite's back end as packets of poop called scybala (SIGH-bah-lah). Just imagine what it'd be like to have lumps of mite-y manure smeared across your skin!

DAISY PARROTFISH

A SLIMY SLEEPING BAG

IF YOU'VE EVER GONE FISHING, there's one thing you know for sure: A fish's body is slick and slippery.

Why do they make all that slimy stuff? So harmful bacteria slide right off their skin. The gooey mucus also makes their scales more flexible.

Some parrotfish depend on their slimy coat for another reason: It helps them sleep soundly. At bedtime, daisy parrotfish cover themselves with a slimy sheath. While the fish rest, the slippery coating keeps tiny bloodsucking isopods away from their bodies.

Does the slimy sack really work? You bet. Parrotfish without cocoons are nine times more likely to be attacked than fish surrounded by slime.

STAT STACK

Habitat: Coral reefs

Size: Up to 16 inches (41 cm) long

Weight: 4 pounds (1.8 kg)

Predators: Moray eels, sharks

Life span: 8 years

🤔 The Name Game

The parrotfish gets its name from its beak-shaped mouth. Its teeth are fused into a superstrong scraper that's perfect for knocking chunks of hard coral off reefs. Why eat coral? To get at the tasty algae living inside.

As parrotfish munch on coral, bones in their throats grind it into sand. The sand passes through the fish's body and, eventually, some of it forms new beaches.

About 80 different species of parrotfish live on Earth today. It can be hard to tell which species a parrotfish belongs to because the color of each fish's skin changes throughout its life.

😖 EXTRA ICK!

What happens to a daisy parrotfish's protective wrapper in the morning? It becomes breakfast! Eating the cocoon helps the fish recoup precious nutrients, so it can use them again.

How does a daisy parrotfish make its nifty nocturnal net? **GLANDS NEAR ITS GILLS PRODUCE THE MUCUS.** Then the slimy stuff slowly surrounds the fish's body. The whole process takes about an hour.

AFRICAN LUNGFISH

A COZY COCOON

MOST FISH USE GILLS TO REMOVE OXYGEN FROM THEIR WATERY WORLD. But as you might guess from its name, the African lungfish also has lungs. And it's a good thing, too.

During the dry season, the shallow, swampy pools lungfish call home slowly evaporate. Going, going, gone! If lungfish couldn't breathe air, they'd be dead meat.

How does a lungfish keep its body moist in a waterless world? First, it nestles into the cool mud. Then a thin layer of gooey mucus oozes out of its body, forming a cozy cocoon. The lungfish rests inside its leathery lair until the rain returns.

STAT STACK

Habitat: Swamps, small rivers

Size: 40 inches (102 cm) long

Weight: 8 pounds (3.6 kg)

Predators: Birds

Life span: 20 to 25 years

🤔 What's for Dinner?

During the rainy season, African lungfish chow down on everything from insects and worms to frogs and other fish. They'll even eat tree roots and seeds.

African lungfish have two different ways of searching for prey. Sometimes they swim-slither through the water. But they can also creep along the bottom using their fins like legs.

Scientists think lungfish are closely related to the first four-legged animals that walked on land.

While an African lungfish is inside its mucus cocoon, it takes a break. **AS IT RESTS, ITS HEART BEATS MORE SLOWLY AND IT BARELY BREATHES.** Believe it or not, the fish can spend more than a year chilling out inside its moist home.

🤢 EXTRA ICK!

Imagine being locked in a room for months with nothing to eat. Seriously. Nothing. Not even a bug. What would you do? You'd starve to death.

But an African lungfish survives inside its wrapper by digesting some of the muscle tissue in its tail. Luckily, the tissue grows back when the fish starts to eat again.

BONE-HOUSE WASP

A BRILLIANT BARRICADE

IN 2014, SCIENTISTS DISCOVERED AN INSECT WITH A VERY STRANGE HABIT. The bone-house wasp stuffs dead ants into the space between the two outermost walls of its nest. That's right—it's like having a front hallway crammed with corpses!

Puzzled by this bizarre behavior? Scientists were, too—until they spent some time studying the nests. Now they believe that chemicals in the ants' bodies make other kinds of wasps think twice about attacking the nest. What are these enemy wasps after? They'd like to lay their own eggs on or in the bone-house wasps' eggs, larvae, or pupae.

The ants' aroma may make other wasps think a predator is present. Or it may hide the scent of the bone-house wasps. Either way, it's a nifty trick.

STAT STACK

Habitat: Mountain forests

Size: 0.5 inch (1.3 cm) long

Weight: Unknown

Predators: Other wasps

Life span: Unknown

WALL

DEAD ANTS

PLANT STEM

WALL

WALL

DEVELOPING PUPA

Adult bone-house wasps **DINE ON POLLEN** and nectar.

🤔 Layers of Larvae

A female bone-house wasp builds her nest one step at a time:

1. After finding a hollow plant stem, the wasp flies off in search of a spider.

2. She paralyzes the prey, drags it back to her nest, and eats its legs so it can't escape.

3. She lays an egg on top of the spider. It'll make a good meal when the little larva hatches.

4. The wasp builds a wall to seal the room, trapping the living spider in a dark, dreary grave.

5. She repeats this process until she's laid all of her eggs.

6. She stuffs up to 13 ants between the outer walls of her nest.

🤢 EXTRA ICK!

What does a female bone-house wasp use to build the walls in her nest? Slimy spit mixed with soil.

FLESH FLY

A TOAD-AL SURPRISE

YOU MAY THINK YOU KNOW WHAT HAPPENS WHEN A FLY AND A TOAD CROSS PATHS, but get ready for a big surprise!

When a female *Lepidodexia bufonivora* flesh fly encounters a harlequin toad, she doesn't become lunch. Instead, she darts down and deposits her newly hatched maggots on the toad's skin.

What happens next? The white, wormy youngsters get to work. They wriggle and squirm as they burrow into the toad's body. After they settle into their safe, snug home, the maggots devour the toad from the inside out.

That's right: In this scenario, the toad croaks.

With their bellies full, the maggots turn into pupae. And a few weeks later, they emerge as adults.

 STAT STACK

Habitat: Tropical rainforests

Size: 0.5 inch (1.3 cm) long

Weight: 0.1 ounce (2.8 g)

Predators: Unknown

Life span: 3 to 5 weeks

A developing *Lepidodexia bufonivora* flesh fly spends between 21 and 37 days inside a harlequin toad.

🤔 A Flesh Fly's Life

Like other flies, flesh flies have a four-stage life cycle. Depending on the temperature of their habitat, the flesh flies that attack harlequin toads spend:

- 1 to 2 days as eggs
- 4 to 7 days as maggots (larvae)
- 17 to 30 days as pupae
- 1 to 2 days as adults

For these short-lived insects, time really flies.

About 2,500 flesh fly species live on Earth today. Most of them look like this one. A female *Lepidodexia bulfonivora* FLESH FLY PRODUCES ABOUT TWO DOZEN MAGGOTS AT A TIME. It takes the larvae about one week to devour a harlequin toad.

🤢 EXTRA ICK!

What do adult flesh flies eat? Sometimes they lap up flower nectar or juices from rotting fruits, but they also feast on fluids in dung and rotting corpses. *Yum!*

DISGUSTING DEFENSES

YOU WON'T BELIEVE HOW SOME ANIMALS STAY SAFE!

An assassin bug carries a dead-ant backpack to fool hungry jumping spiders.

SILVER-SPOTTED SKIPPER CATERPILLAR

FLING THAT FRASS!

WHAT'S FRASS? IT'S A POLITE WAY TO SAY "POOP."
Caterpillar poop, that is.

Caterpillars are eating-and-growing machines. Day and night, rain and shine, nothing stops them from gorging on luscious leaves. And the more they eat, the more they poop.

If a silver-spotted skipper caterpillar's stinky scat were to pile up in one spot ... *Pee-eeew!* The little insect would be an easy target for hungry hunters.

Luckily, the caterpillar has a nifty trick for spreading its scat. It pumps extra blood into its anus. The pressure builds up, up, up until ... *Pop!* A pellet of poop blasts through the air. It can travel more than five feet (1.5 m).

STAT STACK

Habitat: Meadows, swamps

Size: 2 inches (5 cm) long

Weight: Unknown

Predators: Wasps, ants, birds, frogs, spiders

Life span: About 2 months

When a hungry bird plucks a silver-spotted skipper caterpillar off a leaf, the caterpillar fights back. **IT UPCHUCKS A BITTER-TASTING GREENISH LUMP INTO ITS ENEMY'S MOUTH.** *Blech!* The slushy slop tastes so terrible that the bird spits the caterpillar out and searches for a new meal.

🤔 The Name Game

How did skipper butterflies get their name? From the way they fly. The petite insects dodge and dart, skip and dip, flitting across the sky with herky-jerky motions.

When a silver-spotted skipper butterfly lands on a plant, it uncoils its long strawlike proboscis and sips sugary nectar from flowers.

🤢 EXTRA ICK!

Instead of firing frass to get rid of it, a chocolate sailor caterpillar puts its poop to good use.

While chowing down, the caterpillar carefully nibbles around a leaf's central vein. Later, when it relieves itself, the caterpillar attaches its poop pellets to the leaf vein with strands of silk. Over time, the frass covers and surrounds the leaf vein.

Why build such a strange structure? Because it's a safe spot for the caterpillar to hang out. Hungry ants and spiders won't set foot on the frass.

DEFENSES

Disgusting Defenses **73**

KOMODO DRAGON

PROTECTED BY POOP

THE KOMODO DRAGON IS THE LARGEST LIZARD ON EARTH. What does this hulking hunter eat? Anything it can catch—including smaller Komodo dragons! Believe it or not, a hungry grown-up won't even think twice about snacking on its own offspring.

With no one to trust, how does a helpless youngster stay safe? By taking to the trees—one place huge, heavy Komodo dragons can't go.

But once in a while, a youngster needs to come to the ground. That's when it does something surprising: It rolls in its own poop. The awful odor makes even the biggest, hungriest Komodo dragon lose its appetite.

STAT STACK

Habitat: Forests, grasslands

Size: 10 feet (3 m) long

Weight: Up to 330 pounds (150 kg)

Predators: Larger Komodo dragons

Life span: 30 years

As a Komodo dragon ambles along, it flicks its long, forked tongue in and out. Tiny sensors smell and taste the air, leading the reptile to its dinner.

When an adult Komodo dragon catches a youngster by surprise, **THE LITTLE ONE UPCHUCKS ITS LAST MEAL.** Lightening its load makes it easier for the smaller reptile to scurry up a tree.

🤔 On the Hunt

Most of the time, a Komodo dragon dines on deer, water buffalo, or wild boar. When it spots a potential meal, it lunges forward and grabs the prey by the throat.

The massive reptile also feasts on rotting carcasses. It can sniff out a dead or dying animal more than two miles (3.2 km) away.

🤢 EXTRA ICK!

What does a tiny three-lined potato beetle larva have in common with a Komodo dragon? A disgusting defense. To avoid being eaten, the beetle covers its body with its own excrement. Not only does the poop smell bad, it's also poisonous to predators.

NORTHERN SHOVELER

A DUCK'S DUNG DEFENSE

SCRATCH. SCUFF. SCRAPE. Each spring, a female northern shoveler makes a shallow hole in the ground. She lines it with grass. Then she plucks soft, downy feathers from her body and adds them to her nest.

After laying 8 to 12 eggs, the female duck sits and waits. And waits. And waits. It takes more than three weeks for the eggs to hatch.

What happens if a hungry red fox sneaks up on the nest? The frantic female quickly protects her eggs by spraying them with poop. Then she takes flight. When the coast is clear, the duck returns to her nest.

STAT STACK

Habitat: Open wetlands

Size: 19 inches (48 cm) long

Weight: 1 pound (0.5 kg)

Predators: Red foxes, weasels, martens, raccoons

Life span: 15 to 20 years

A female northern shoveler's **CAMOUFLAGED COLORING HELPS HER BLEND IN WITH HER SURROUNDINGS,** but on calm days, some predators may be able to sniff her out.

🤔 The Name Game

How did the northern shoveler get its name? From the shape of its bill. It may look strange, but the shovel-shaped beak is perfect for filtering seeds, insects, and tiny fingernail clams out of muddy water.

At feeding time, the duck zooms across the surface of the water like a vacuum cleaner. As water flows through its wide, flat bill, comblike projections on its tongue snag tasty tidbits.

A northern shoveler uses its beak to filter seeds and small animals out of the water.

🤢 EXTRA ICK!

Common eiders are bigger than northern shovelers, and they live on ocean shores. But when a hungry hunter attacks, they depend on the same disgusting defense. They shower their eggs with scat to keep predators away. *Pee-eeew!*

SIBERIAN CHIPMUNK

PROTECTED BY PEE

THE SIBERIAN CHIPMUNK LIVES IN THE DEEP, DARK FOREST, and it has more than its fair share of predators. Snakes. Hawks. Owls. Weasels. Foxes. They're all happy to dine on tasty chipmunk meat.

That would be bad news for some little critters. But the Siberian chipmunk has a nifty trick for avoiding its enemies: When it spots a dead snake, it uses its teeth to slice open the reptile's bladder. After all the urine drains onto the ground, the chipmunk takes a bath in the stinky pee. Gross!

Think the chipmunk is nuts? Think again. The snake's strong scent keeps predators away.

STAT STACK

Habitat: Forests

Size: 4 to 6 inches (10 to 15 cm) long

Weight: 3 to 5 ounces (85 to 142 g)

Predators: Hawks, owls, snakes, weasels, foxes

Life span: 2 to 5 years

Siberian chipmunks have no trouble climbing trees, but **THEY SPEND MOST OF THEIR TIME SCURRYING ALONG THE GROUND** in search of seeds, nuts, mushrooms, berries, and insects.

🤔 Getting Ready for Winter

Each autumn, a Siberian chipmunk collects up to eight pounds (3.6 kg) of food to eat during the long, cold winter. Where does it store all those tasty treats? In an underground burrow.

Its home can be up to five feet (1.5 m) deep and seven feet (2.1 m) long. Besides food storage rooms, the burrow has a nest room and a toilet room.

When a Siberian chipmunk's cheek pouches are full, each one can be one and a half times bigger than its head!

🤢 EXTRA ICK!

Siberian chipmunks also gnaw on snakeskin and nibble on snake scat. Then they rub the chewed-up material on their fur. It's another way to cover up their own aroma with the snake's scary smell.

MORAFKA'S DESERT TORTOISE

PICK A TRICK

WHAT'S THE FIRST THING YOU NOTICE when you look at a Morafka's desert tortoise? Its shell, of course. The hard, heavy home protects its owner from a parade of predators.

But the shell is no match for a cougar's giant teeth or a golden eagle's sharp talons. What can the tortoise do when it senses these enemies? Freeze! As long as it stays still, the predator may mistake it for a rock.

And if that doesn't work, the resourceful reptile has another trick up its, er, shell: If an enemy grabs it, the tortoise relieves itself. That's right! It pees on its predator. Yuck! That's enough to make any enemy skedaddle.

STAT STACK

Habitat: Sonoran Desert

Size: 10 to 14 inches (25 to 36 cm) long

Weight: Up to 11 pounds (5 kg)

Predators: Coyotes, cougars, golden eagles

Life span: Up to 80 years

A Morafka's desert tortoise **CAN SURVIVE IN SWELTERING DESERT AREAS ON THE HOTTEST SUMMER DAYS.** It gets all the water it needs from its food, which includes grasses and cactus fruits and flowers.

🤔 Home Sweet Home

How do Morafka's desert tortoises beat the heat? By seeking shelter. These master diggers can build burrows up to six feet (1.8 m) deep. They spend about 95 percent of their lives resting in their cool, moist dens.

The entrance to a Morafka's desert tortoise's burrow is often under a rocky outcrop.

🤢 EXTRA ICK!

After a female tortoise lays 4 to 12 eggs, she buries them and pees on the pile. The stinky urine prevents hungry foxes and lizards from smelling the eggs.

DEFENSES

PACIFIC HAGFISH

IT'S SLIME TIME!

WHAT HAS FIVE HEARTS BUT NO STOMACH?
What can sense the scent of rotting fish from a mile (1.6 km) away but can barely see a thing? The Pacific hagfish.

This strange creature spends its days creeping along the ocean floor in search of sea worms and other tasty morsels. When it comes across a dying fish, it slithers inside and eats the helpless victim from the inside out.

Think that's gross? Wait until you hear how a hagfish protects itself from enemies. When a bigger fish attacks, gooey gobs of slippery slime ooze out of a hagfish's skin. The icky, sticky mucus traps the enemy and clogs its gills, making it hard for it to breathe. While the hapless hunter fights to get free, the hagfish swims to safety.

STAT STACK

Habitat: Muddy ocean bottom

Size: 17 inches (43 cm) long

Weight: 2 to 3 pounds (0.9 to 1.4 kg)

Predators: Sharks and other large fish, harbor seals

Life span: 40 years

A Pacific hagfish has about 200 slime pores running the length of its body. **THEY RELEASE THREADLIKE FIBERS OF MUCUS THAT SWELL INTO THICK, SNOTTY SLIME** the instant they hit seawater.

SLIME PORE

🤔 A Blast From the Past

Hagfish have lived on Earth for at least 300 million years. That means they were swimming in Earth's oceans for 70 million years before the first dinosaurs appeared.

These primitive creatures don't have bones or teeth. Instead, they have toothlike structures made of the same material as your fingernails.

Even though a hagfish doesn't have true teeth, it can still munch on sea worms and scrape meat off dead fish.

🤢 EXTRA ICK!

As hagfish feed on a large carcass, such as a dead whale, they release mucus into the seawater. In just a few minutes, it forms a cloud of slime that prevents other animals from joining the feast.

DEEP-SEA OSTRACOD

A BURST OF BLUE

DOWN, DOWN IN THE DEPTHS OF THE OCEAN, a little bit of light can be a *really* big deal. And deep-sea ostracods know it. That's why these teeny-tiny critters have a brilliant trick for staying safe.

The instant an ostracod is eaten by a hungry cardinalfish, it produces slimy glow-in-the-dark mucus that lights up the fish's body. Yikes! The shocked fish upchucks the ostracod and spits it into the water. After all, the fish has predators of its own. The last thing it needs is a bright blue light that says, *Here's dinner! Come and get it.*

As the ostracod exits, it keeps making mucus. It may even swim in circles around the cardinalfish, drawing more attention to its enemy.

STAT STACK

Habitat: Deep ocean

Size: 0.4 inch (1 cm) long

Weight: Unknown

Predators: Cardinalfish, trumpetfish, horse mackerel, lanternfish

Life span: Unknown

CARDINALFISH

Most of an ostracod's saclike body is filled with water, but it has two large eyes (top), a strong heart, and a digestive tract to break down its food.

A deep-sea **OSTRACOD** (below) **RACES AWAY FROM A CARDINALFISH** (above) that has just spewed it out into the water.

🤔 Eye See You

Thanks to a transparent outer shell, it's easy to see what's inside a deep-sea ostracod's body.

Two large golden eyes help the petite predator spot prey in very dim light. What does it eat? Even smaller critters, including copepods, arrow worms, and newly hatched fish.

🤢 EXTRA ICK!

What does a deep-sea ostracod have in common with a freshwater snail called the Latia limpet? Glimmering goo! When a hungry fish attacks, greenish yellow mucus oozes out of the limpet's body. As water currents carry the slimy stuff away, the confused fish follows the trail of glowing light. So long, sucker!

DEEP-SEA OSTRACOD

VIRGINIA OPOSSUM

THE FURRY FAKER

THINK THIS VIRGINIA OPOSSUM LOOKS DEAD? YOU AREN'T ALONE. That's what most predators would think, too. But it's all a trick.

Seriously. The furry faker could win an award for its acting—it's that convincing.

An opossum can't run fast, and it doesn't blend in with its surroundings, so when the little critter senses danger, it flops on its side and plays dead. Its heart slows down. So does its breathing. Green slime may ooze out of its body, smelling like a rotting corpse.

Most hungry hunters are looking for fresh meat. By playing dead, an opossum fools predators into thinking it's a bad meal choice.

STAT STACK

Habitat: Forests, fields, swamps

Size: 28 to 30 inches (71 to 76 cm) long

Weight: 4 to 7 pounds (1.8 to 3.2 kg)

Predators: Foxes, coyotes, hawks, owls

Life span: 2 years

🤔 Packed in a Pouch

Opossums are the only marsupials that live in North America. Like their kangaroo and koala relatives, they're born blind and furless. The first thing they do is crawl across their mom's fur to the pouch on her belly. It's a harrowing trip for babies the size of black beans! Young opossums stay inside the protective pouch for about two months. Then they spend another four to six weeks hitching a ride on their mom's back.

This furry family gives new meaning to the word "backpack." A mama opossum can carry as many as 13 youngsters everywhere she goes.

A Virginia opossum can **PLAY DEAD** for up to six hours.

🤢 EXTRA ICK!

An opossum will eat almost anything, including fruit, insects, earthworms, bird eggs, baby birds, frogs, and snakes. But it doesn't stop there. It also raids garbage cans and dines on rotting roadkill.

TEXAS HORNED LIZARD

SQUIRT ALERT!

A TEXAS HORNED LIZARD MAY BE SMALL, BUT IT SURE KNOWS HOW TO SURVIVE. When it senses danger, it darts across the desert.

Then it suddenly stops and flattens its body against the ground. The lizard's sand-colored scales make it hard to spot.

If that doesn't fool the enemy, the lizard hisses fiercely. It puffs up its body to twice its normal size. It may even jab at its attacker with its horns and spines.

What if the hungry hunter still doesn't give up? No worries. The lizard has one more trick: It squirts a stream of blood out of the corners of its eyes. Yikes! As the startled predator backs away, the lizard makes its escape.

STAT STACK

Habitat: Deserts, scrublands

Size: 2 to 4 inches (5 to 10 cm) long

Weight: 1 to 3 ounces (28 to 85 g)

Predators: Hawks, owls, roadrunners, snakes, coyotes, bobcats

Life span: 5 to 8 years

A horned lizard can shoot blood from its eyes up to three feet (1 m). It usually aims for its enemy's mouth because the blood tastes terrible.

A Texas horned lizard **SPENDS MOST MORNINGS BASKING IN THE SUN.** Its sand-colored scales help it blend in with its surroundings.

🤔 A Drop to Drink

Rain is rare in the hot, dry desert, so when a storm strikes, a Texas horned lizard is ready. It arches its broad back to catch as many drops as possible. When it lowers its head, water flows down channels between its scales, trickling into the little lizard's mouth.

🤢 EXTRA ICK!

Believe it or not, the Texas horned lizard isn't the only animal that relies on its blood to stay safe. When a predator snaps up a blister beetle ... *Ouch!* A chemical in the beetle's blood makes the attacker's mouth burn. If the predator doesn't spit the insect out, painful blisters form in its mouth and throat.

desert blister beetle

Disgusting Defenses   **89**

NORTHERN FULMAR

A SHOWER OF STINKY SPLATTER

WHEN NORTHERN FULMAR PARENTS FLY OFF IN SEARCH OF FISH, THEIR SINGLE TINY CHICK MUST FEND FOR ITSELF. Luckily, the baby bird is anything but helpless.

When a gull or broad-winged skua approaches the nest, the little one opens its beak wide and showers the attacker with a stream of bright orange, fishy-smelling spew. *Thwack.* The chick can fire half a dozen blasts in quick succession and hit a moving target up to six feet (1.8 m) away.

The oily vomit sticks to a predator's feathers, making it hard to fly. The puke can also destroy the waterproof coating on an attacker's feathers, and that's bad news for birds that spend their whole lives in and around the ocean.

STAT STACK

Habitat: Ocean coastlines

Size: 18 inches (46 cm) long

Weight: 1 to 2 pounds (0.5 to 0.9 kg)

Predators: Other seabirds

Life span: 32 years

A northern fulmar chick on the Shetland Islands in Scotland **DEFENDS ITSELF BY SPRAYING PREDATORS** with a nasty, oily liquid.

🤔 Sniff, Sniff, Take a Whiff!

Birds don't have a nose sticking out of their head like you do, but they do have two nostrils. These holes take in air. They pick up scents, too.

Most birds don't have a good sense of smell, but the northern fulmar does. That's how it finds fish and other tasty treats as it flies through the air. Then it drops down to the ocean's surface and snatches its meal.

A fulmar has two tubelike nostrils that sit atop its beak. They help the bird smell squids, shrimps, jellyfish, and dead carcasses.

🤢 EXTRA ICK!

Like fulmar chicks, young European rollers spew putrid puke if their parents are away and they sense danger. But instead of targeting their enemy, they spray themselves. The nasty odor makes the baby birds a less attractive snack.

An adult European roller returns to its nest with food.

BLACK-NECKED SPITTING COBRA

SPIT-ACULAR SNAKES

LOTS OF SNAKES HAVE FANGS, BUT ONLY SPITTING COBRAS CAN USE THEM TO SPRAY VENOM.

When a large animal, such as a wildebeest gets too close, the scared snake rises up, spreads its hood, and opens its mouth wide. A muscle behind the snake's eyes squeezes a sac full of venom, forcing the toxic fluid into the snake's fangs and thrusting it out of a tiny hole at the tip of each tooth.

The snake aims for the larger animal's eyes and hits its target about 80 percent of the time. The venom causes a painful burning that sends its recipient running.

STAT STACK

Habitat: Grasslands, scrublands

Size: 4 to 7 feet (1.2 to 2.1 m) long

Weight: 15 to 20 pounds (6.8 to 9 kg)

Predators: Snake eagles, monitor lizards, mongooses, crocodiles

Life span: 20 years

A black-necked spitting cobra uses its forked tongue to sense prey.

A black-necked spitting cobra **CAN SPIT VENOM EIGHT FEET** (2.4 m). The nasty spray can cause swelling, blisters, and even blindness.

🤔 What's for Dinner?

A spitting cobra spits when it feels threatened but not when hunger strikes. To catch prey, the snake hides in a hole or below a bush. When a mouse, bird, or lizard passes by, the hunter lunges forward and seizes the prey with its fangs. As venom flows into the victim's body, the animal becomes paralyzed.

What happens next? The cobra unhinges its jaw and slowly swallows its meal.

🤢 EXTRA ICK!

Spitting snakes aren't the only animals that protect themselves by spouting noxious spray. But there's one important difference: Skunks, zorillas, bombardier beetles (see pages 94–95), and wood ants all fire their noxious liquids from their rear ends.

baby skunk

Disgusting Defenses **93**

ASIAN BOMBARDIER BEETLE

A SLIMY ESCAPE

ONCE UPON A TIME, THERE WAS A BEETLE AND A TOAD. As you might expect, the hungry Japanese common toad flicked its tongue, nabbed the insect, and swallowed it down. *Gulp!*

Think that's the end of this true tale? Then you're in for a surprise.

More than an hour later, the toad upchucked its meal in a ball of gooey mucus, and the slime-covered beetle slowly crawled away.

How'd that happen? Our little hero—the Asian bombardier beetle—didn't give up. It fought back by blasting the toad's insides with a nasty, sizzling-hot spray. Finally, the toad couldn't take it anymore and spewed its supper.

STAT STACK

Habitat: Fields, forests

Size: 0.8 inch (2 cm)

Weight: Unknown

Predators: Ants, frogs, spiders

Life span: Several weeks

This Japanese common toad barfed up the Asian bombardier beetle 88 minutes after eating it. Scientists could hear cracking sounds inside the toad every time the beetle sprayed its enemy.

🤔 Hot Stuff!

The scalding spray a bombardier beetle fires out its rear end is almost as hot as boiling water. Why doesn't the insect burn itself? Because the spray has two ingredients, and they're stored in separate sacs inside the beetle's body. The two chemicals don't mix until they're exiting into the air.

😨 EXTRA ICK!

As soon as a bombardier beetle larva hatches, it needs to start looking for food. What's its meal of choice? The pupa of another kind of beetle. The larva crawls inside the helpless pupa and eats its victim from the inside out.

An Asian bombardier beetle sprays chemicals at a predator. The beetle **CAN FIRE ABOUT 20 TIMES BEFORE IT HAS TO TAKE A BREAK** to let its body produce more chemicals.

MALAYSIAN CARPENTER ANT

ENEMY ANT ....•

PACKED WITH POISON

A MALAYSIAN CARPENTER ANT MAY BE SMALL, BUT THAT DOESN'T MEAN IT ISN'T DEADLY. Two sacs packed with poison stretch the length of her body.

When other ants attack, the carpenter ant prepares to protect her colony. As she squeezes the muscles along her abdomen, pressure builds up inside her body until ... *Kaboom!* The ant explodes, and poison blasts out in every direction.

The sticky spray clings to the enemy ants' legs and jaws. It may even glue the invaders in place. Within minutes, the enemy ants are dead. And so is the carpenter ant. She has lost her life defending her family and their home.

STAT STACK

Habitat: Rainforests

Size: Up to 1 inch (2.5 cm) long

Weight: Unknown

Predators: Weaver ants, spiders

Life span: 6 to 12 weeks

CICADA HEAD

Malaysian carpenter ants
feed on a green cicada (center)
in their rainforest home.

MALAYSIAN
CARPENTER ANT

🤔 Home Sweet Home

Malaysian carpenter ants live in moist, rotting wood. They use their strong jaws to build a network of tunnels.

At night, the ants march out in search of food. When they find a dead insect, they suck it dry. Then they look for more. When the ants go home, they upchuck part of their meal to feed their queen and all the little larvae.

😣 EXTRA ICK!

Believe it or not, some termites explode, too. As their bodies are blown to bits, a sticky yellow liquid gushes out.

Most of the ants in a colony are females. They dig tunnels, take care of youngsters, collect food, and guard their home. **MALAYSIAN CARPENTER ANTS THAT GUARD THE COLONY'S NEST HAVE POISON SACS** that extend from their jaws to the tip of their abdomen.

WESTERN HOOKNOSE SNAKE

BLASTS OF GAS!

THHHHHHP! WHAT'S THAT SOUND?

No, it's not a fellow hiker tooting up a storm. It's a western hooknose snake sending you an important message: *Watch out! Don't step on me!*

When the slithering serpent feels frightened, it lets one rip. Seriously. It sounds just like a fart.

To produce its warning toots, a western hooknose snake forces a stream of air bubbles out its back end. As the gas gushes out, the walls of the snake's cloaca vibrate back and forth. Sometimes the blast of gas is so strong that the snake's whole body shoots up into the air and then crashes back down.

 STAT STACK

Habitat: Scrublands, grasslands

Size: 7 to 11 inches (18 to 28 cm) long

Weight: Unknown

Predators: Foxes, coyotes, hawks

Life span: Unknown

🤔 The Name Game

As you might have guessed, the western hooknose snake gets its name from its upturned, hook-like snout. The snake's nifty nose is perfect for plowing through loose, sandy soil as it tunnels underground.

Like all snakes, the western hooknose snake uses its forked tongue—not the nostrils on its snout—to pick up scents from the air.

Western hooknose snakes usually **REST UNDERGROUND DURING THE DAY.** At night, they hunt for spiders, scorpions, insects, and centipedes.

🤢 EXTRA ICK!

When a Sonoran coral snake is about to strike, it makes a farting sound—just like a western hooknose snake. Each pop is quicker than the blink of an eye, and the sound can be heard from up to six feet (1.8 m) away.

TWO-SPOTTED SARDINE

FEROCIOUS FISH

AT FIRST GLANCE, TWO-SPOTTED SARDINES SEEM INNOCENT ENOUGH. These silvery swimmers spend their days traveling in groups called schools. Some pluck tasty tidbits out of the water. Others nibble on rotting material that blankets the bottom.

But when a hungry wolffish lurks nearby, the mild-mannered sardines suddenly get nasty. They target one of their own ... and attack. Then they force the injured sardine out of the school, making it an easy target for the predator.

As the lucky wolffish enjoys its meal, the rest of the sardines swim out of sight.

STAT STACK

Habitat: Rivers, streams, ponds, swamps

Size: 6 to 7 inches (15 to 18 cm) long

Weight: 3 ounces (85 g)

Predators: Larger fish, herons

Life span: 18 years

🤔 Fish Fry Feeding Frenzy

A female two-spotted sardine can produce up to 10,000 eggs, and she releases them into the water all at once. The eggs hatch in less than a day. And after just a few hours, the tiny fry start swimming.

At first, the growing fish are able to find food. But when it runs out, they turn on each other. When the feeding frenzy is over, only a few hundred sardines are left.

As adults, two-spotted sardines live in schools with about 50 members.

Some people keep **TWO-SPOTTED SARDINES AS PETS.** As long as there are no predators in the fish tank, the sardines won't attack one another.

😰 EXTRA ICK!

Think two-spotted sardines are the only animals that attack one another to increase their odds of survival? Think again. At least 1,300 kinds of animals, including hamsters, polar bears, and chimpanzees, kill other members of their species so they'll have a better chance of surviving.

ASSASSIN BUG

A DISGUSTING DISGUISE

WHEN A HUNGRY ASSASSIN BUG SPOTS AN ANT, IT ATTACKS. First, it jabs its victim with its sharp mouthparts. Then it paralyzes the prey with spit. As the ant's insides turn to mush, the assassin bug sucks up the juices.

What happens to the leftovers? The assassin bug attaches the ant's empty exoskeleton to its back. Each time the hunter eats an ant, it adds the carcass to the stack on its back. Over time, the ants slowly pile up, up, up.

Imagine lugging around a hulking heap of dead ants. Seems strange, right? But the mound of corpses is actually a clever disguise. It changes the assassin bug's overall shape, so that hungry jumping spiders don't recognize it as prey.

STAT STACK

Habitat: Forests, grasslands

Size: 0.4 inch (1 cm) long

Weight: Unknown

Predators: Jumping spiders

Life span: Unknown

As you can tell from this jumping spider's raised front legs, it does not like to be around ants.

🤔 The Ant-i-Spider Solution

Carcass-carrying assassin bugs hunt beetles and flies as well as ants, but they don't pile these other insects onto their backs. Scientists think there's a good reason for that: Jumping spiders don't like ants. In fact, they avoid ants whenever they can. Even in a jumbled pile, the empty corpses may still drive the spiders away.

An assassin bug can carry as many as 20 empty ant carcasses on its back. It **BINDS THEM TOGETHER WITH A STICKY SUBSTANCE** that oozes out of its body.

🤢 EXTRA ICK!

Assassin bugs aren't the only insects that depend on disgusting disguises. Swallowtail caterpillars camouflage themselves as poop. That's right: Their bodies look just like bird droppings. As long as the little larvae stay perfectly still, predators leave them alone.

DEFENSES

CONCLUSION

THIS ISN'T THE END!

FINISHING THIS BOOK MEANS YOU HAVE A CURIOUS MIND—AND A STRONG STOMACH. Congratulations! You're a real champ. You've read more than 16,000 words and learned about dozens of amazing animals. It's hard to believe how many creatures do something that plenty of people would consider pretty darn gross. But believe it or not, this isn't the end. It's really just the beginning.

Scientists identify and name at least 15,000 new species every single year. They're also learning more about well-known animals all the time. So keep your eyes peeled for more fascinating finds in the future.

And who knows? If you stay curious and pay attention, you could be the one who does the discovering.

GLOSSARY

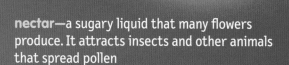

THORAX

ABDOMEN

abdomen—the back section of an insect's body

anus—the hole through which poop exits the body

bacterium (plural: bacteria)—a tiny, one-celled living thing that reproduces by splitting in half

bladder—a body part that collects urine before it leaves the body

carcass—the dead body of an animal

cecotrope—a soft, shiny pellet full of partially digested food

cloaca—in some animals, a multipurpose opening at the rear of the body

colony—a group of animals that live together

dwelling—the place where an animal lives

echolocation—detecting objects by sending out sounds and gathering information from the timing and characteristics of the echo

evaporate—to change from a liquid to a gas

exoskeleton—the hard, protective outer layer that covers the bodies of insects, spiders, and other arthropods

feces—animal waste material; poop

grub—the second stage in the life of most beetles and bees

incisor—a front tooth that cuts through hard foods, such as plants

larva (plural: larvae)—the second stage in the life of amphibians and many arthropods

maggot—the second stage in the life cycle of most flies

molar—a large, wide tooth at the back of an animal's mouth

molt—to shed an old exoskeleton that is too small

mucus—a slimy mixture produced by an animal's body

nectar—a sugary liquid that many flowers produce. It attracts insects and other animals that spread pollen

nostril—one of the holes that take in air, allowing land animals to breathe and, in some creatures, smell

nutrient—a substance that keeps the body healthy. It comes from food.

nymph—the second stage in the life of some insects

offspring—babies or young animals

paralyze—to make an animal unable to move

parasite—a creature that lives on another creature and uses it as food

poison—a substance that can cause sickness or death if a creature touches it, breathes it in, or eats it

pupa (plural: pupae)—the third stage in the life of some insects

regurgitate—to bring up partially digested food

ruminant—a plant-eating animal that chews cud regurgitated from its stomach

saliva—a watery liquid produced in an animal's mouth

scat—animal waste material; poop

thorax—the middle section of an insect's body, where the legs are attached

venom—a harmful liquid that some animals make inside their bodies and inject into predators or prey

SELECTED SOURCES

*Amazing Animals of the World, Set 1, Volumes 1–10. Danbury, CT: Grolier/Scholastic, 2008.

*Amazing Animals of the World, Set 2, Volumes 1–10. Danbury, CT: Grolier/Scholastic, 2005.

*Amazing Animals of the World, Set 3, Volumes 1–10. Danbury, CT: Grolier/Scholastic, 2006.

Animal Diversity Web, animaldiversity.org.

Attenborough, David. Life in Cold Blood. Princeton, NJ: Princeton University Press, 2008.

Attenborough, David. The Life of Mammals. Princeton, NJ: Princeton University Press, 2002.

Attenborough, David. Trials of Life: A Natural History of Behavior. NY: Little, Brown, 1990.

*Bardoe, Cheryl. Behold the Beautiful Dung Beetle. Watertown, MA: Charlesbridge, 2014.

Barrat, John. "Scientists in Awe of Huge Olfactory Bulb Found in Turkey Vulture Brain." Smithsonian Insider, December 12, 2017. insider.si.edu/2017/12/scientists-in-awe -of-huge-olfactory-bulb-found-in-turkey-vulture-brain.

Bates, Mary. "Tongue-Eating Parasites Inspire New Horror Movie." American Association for the Advancement of Science, September 18, 2012. aaas.org/blog/qualia/ tongue-eating-parasites-inspire-new-horror-movie.

Breed, Michael D., and Janice Moore, eds. Encyclopedia of Animal Behavior. Waltham, MA: Academic Press, 2010.

*Carwardine, Mark. Natural History Museum Book of Animal Records. Richmond Hill, ON, Canada: Firefly Books, 2013.

Chapman, Demian, et al. "The Behavioural and Genetic Mating System of the Sand Tiger Shark, Carcharias taurus, an Intrauterine Cannibal." Biology Letters 9, no. 3. June 23, 2013. royalsocietypublishing.org/doi/10.1098/ rsbl.2013.0003.

Crew, Becky. "New Skin-Feeding Amphibian Found in French Guiana." Scientific American, April 17, 2013. blogs.scientificamerican.com/running-ponies/ new-skin-feeding-amphibian-found-in-french-guiana.

Crump, M. L., and J. A. Pounds. "Lethal Parasitism of an Aposematic Anuran (Atelopus varius) by Notochaeta bufonivora (Diptera: Sarcophagidae)." Journal of Parasitology 71, no. 5 (1985): 588–91.

Dungl, Eveline, zoological curator and animal trainer, Vienna Zoo, Vienna, Austria, email message to author, January 16, 2019.

"Fish Fireworks: Bioluminescence." Super Senses: The Secret Power of Animals. BBC, August 11, 2014. bbc.co.uk/ programmes/p024m0s1.

Glausiuz, Josie. "A Pop a Day Keeps the Predators Away." Discover, August 1, 2000. discovermagazine.com/2000/ aug/breakpop.

Gomati, V., K. Ramasamy, K. Kumar, N. Sivaramaiah, and R. V. R. Mula. "Greenhouse Gas Emissions From Termite Ecosystem." African Journal of Environmental Science and Technology, 2011. ajol.info/index.php/ajest/article/ view/71907.

Grant, Jacqualine Bonnie. "Diversification of Gut Morphology in Caterpillars Is Associated With Defensive Behavior." Journal of Experimental Biology 209, no. 15 (2006): 3018–24.

Hall, Donald W. "Silver-Spotted Skipper." Featured Creatures. University of Florida Institute of Food and Agricultural Science, June 2011. entnemdept.ufl.edu/creatures/bfly/ silver-spotted_skipper.htm.

*Hirsch, Rebecca E. Exploding Ants and Other Amazing Defenses. Minneapolis, MN: Lerner, 2017.

"The Incredible Termite Mound." PBS, October 28, 2011. pbs.org/wnet/nature/the-animal-house-the -incredible-termite-mound/7222.

*Jenkins, Steve. The Animal Book: A Collection of the Fastest, Fiercest, Toughest, Cleverest, Shyest and Most Surprising Animals on Earth. Boston: Houghton Mifflin Harcourt, 2013.

Johnson, J., and K. Hagen. "A Neuropterous Larva Uses an Allomone to Attack Termites." Nature 289 (1981): 506–07.

*Johnson, Rebecca L. When Lunch Fights Back. Minneapolis, MN: Millbrook Press, 2015.

Kobayashi, Tomomichi. "Behavioral Responses of Siberian Chipmunks Toward Conspecifics Applied Snake Scent." Zoological Science 17, no. 3 (2000): 319–21.

*Kwok, Roberta. "Caecilians: The Other Amphibians." Science News for Students. May 16, 2012. sciencenewsforstudents.org/article/caecilians -other-amphibian.

Levey, Douglas J., R. Scot Duncan, and Carrie F. Levins. "Use of Dung as a Tool by Burrowing Owls." Nature 431 (2004): 39.

SELECTED SOURCES CONTINUED

Margonelli, Lisa. "Collective Mind in the Mound: How Do Termites Build Their Huge Structures?" *National Geographic*, August 1, 2014. news.nationalgeographic .com/news/2014/07/140731-termites-mounds -insects-entomology-science.

Marshall, Michael. "Zoologger: Traitorous Fish Throw Friends to the Wolves." *New Scientist* 219, no. 2926 (2013): 14. newscientist.com/article/dn23852-zoologger-traitorous -fish-throw-friends-to-the-wolves.

McCorquodale, Ariane, Dames P. Cuda, and Sanford D. Porter. "Fire Ant Decapitating Flies." *Featured Creatures.* University of Florida Institute of Food and Agricultural Science, April 2017. entnemdept.ufl.edu/creatures/beneficial/flies/ant_ decapitating_phorids.htm.

Milius, Susan. "Real Vampires of Planet Earth." *Science News* 192, no. 7 (2017): 22–26.

Milius, Susan. "When Mom Serves Herself as Dinner," *Science News*, April 21, 2015.

*"Mother-Eating Spiders." *NatGeo WILD*, January 13, 2014. youtube.com/watch?v=coUd6d3j_6g.

*National Geographic: Animals, nationalgeographic.com/ animals.

Nosowitz, Dan. "Why Thousands of New Animal Species Are Still Discovered Each Year." Atlas Obscura, June 1, 2015. atlasobscura.com/articles/new-animal-species.

Oregon Zoo: Animals, oregonzoo.org/discover/animals.

Schutt, Bill. *Cannibalism.* Chapel Hill, NC: Algonquin Books, 2017.

Simon, Matt. *The Wasp That Brainwashed the Caterpillar: Evolution's Most Unbelievable Solutions to Life's Biggest Problems.* New York: Penguin Books, 2016.

Smith, G., S. T. Trumbo, D. S. Sikes, M. P. Scott, and R. L. Smith. "Host Shift by the Burying Beetle, *Nicrophorus pustulatus*, a Parasitoid of Snake Eggs." *Journal of Evolutionary Biology* 20, no. 6 (2007): 2389–99.

Smithsonian National Zoo: Animals, nationalzoo.si.edu/ animals.

Soniak, Matt. "11 Bloody Facts About Vampire Bats," *Mental Floss*, October 11, 2013. mentalfloss.com/article/ 53128/11-bloody-facts-about-vampire-bats.

Staab, Michael, Michael Oh, Chao-Dong Zhu, and Alexandra-Maria Klein. "A Unique Nest-Protection Strategy in a New Species of Spider Wasp." *PLOS ONE* 9, no. 7 (July 2, 2014): 9–15.

*Stewart, Melissa. *Do People Really Have Tiny Insects Living in Their Eyelashes? And Other Questions About the Microscopic World.* Minneapolis: Lerner, 2011.

*Stewart, Melissa. *How Do Bees Make Honey?* Tarrytown, NY: Marshall Cavendish, 2009.

Stewart, Melissa, personal observations recorded in nature and travel journals, 1989–present.

Stromberg, Joseph. "This Insect Uses Its Victims' Carcasses as Camouflage." *Smithsonian*, May 8, 2012. smithsonianmag.com/science-nature/this-insect-uses -its-victims-carcasses-as-camouflage-83656246.

Sugiura, Shinji, and Takuya Sato. "Successful Escape of Bombardier Beetles From Predator Digestive Systems." *Biology Letters*, February 1, 2018. royalsocietypublishing .org/doi/full/10.1098/rsbl.2017.0647.

"Turkey Vulture." *Canadian Raptor Conservancy.* canadianraptorconservancy.com/birds_vultures_ turkey.php.

Walker, Matt. "Baby Cannibal Spider Gang Makes Web Vibrate in Time." *BBC Earth News*, June 24, 2010. news.bbc.co.uk/earth/hi/earth_news/newsid_8757000/ 8757771.stm.

Weeks, Paul. "Red-Billed Oxpeckers: Vampires or Tickbirds." *Behavioral Ecology* 11, no. 2 (2010): 154–60.

"'Zombie Worms' Found Off Sweden." *BBC News*, October 18, 2005. news.bbc.co.uk/2/hi/4354286.stm.

*Recommended for curious kids.

CREDITS

INDEX